MY SELF-LOVE JOURNAL

This journal belongs to:

_____

WELCOME TO THE SELF-LOVE JOURNAL

♥ ♥ ♥ ♥

Hey there!

Welcome to the self-love journal! This journal was created to give you a special place to write down loving thoughts about yourself.

This journal features a ton of fun prompts and questions that we hope will help you build your self-worth and encourage you to love yourself more.

You can also feel free to add stickers, notes, doodles, or anything else to pages in your journal to make it more fun and interesting.

We truly hope that you enjoy using this journal and that it helps boost your spirits and shows you how awesome you are!

Enjoy!

1. What is your definition of self-love?

....

....

....

....

....

....

....

....

....

....

....

....

Date: ....

2. If you could write a book about self-love, what title would you give it?

BOOK 1

BOOK 2

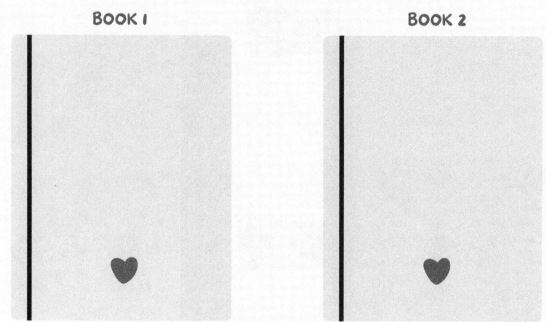

BOOK 3

3. List 3 people you would dedicate your self-love book to and why...

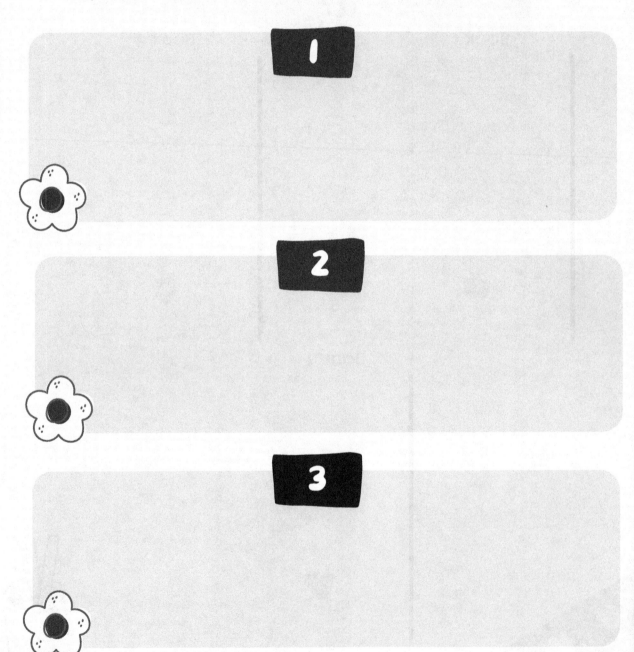

1

2

3

Date: ....

4. What is your biggest talent?

_____

_____

_____

_____

_____

_____

_____

Date: ....

5. What do you love most about your body? List 5 things

#1

#2

#3

#4

#5

ADD SOME

MAGIC *

TO YOUR

LIFE

Date: ....

6. Name 3 of your BIGGEST accomplishments.

Date: ....

7. How would you define self-care?

_____

_____

_____

_____

_____

_____

_____

8. What activities do you like to do for self-care that put you in a good mood?

....

....

....

....

....

....

9. Make a list of your favorite things to do.

10. When I get lost in .... I .... Write your responses below.

....

....

....

....

....

....

....

Date: ....

11. What are your top 5 self-love affirmations?

12. What are 3 things your friends would say they love about you?

1.

2.

3.

FRIENDS FOREVER

13. What is your favorite self-love book and why?

....

....

....

....

....

....

....

Date: ....

14. My favorite singer/musician is _____ because they teach me to love myself by:

....

....

....

....

....

....

....

Date: ....

15. What does a perfect day look like for you?

16. What do you love about yourself?

....

....

....

....

....

....

....

....

SELF love

Date: ....

17. What 3 things do you love to do that bring joy into your life?

1.

2.

3.

18. What form of self-love do you practice?

1.

2.

3.

4.

5.

6.

Date: ....

19. What is the best compliment you've received and how did it make you feel?

....

....

....

....

....

....

....

....

Date: ....

20. When you feel your happiest?

....

....

....

....

....

....

....

....

....

Date: ....

21. If you could travel to the past or your future, where would you go and why?

PASSPORT

Date: ....

22. My greatest accomplishment so far is ......

....

....

....

....

....

....

....

....

....

23. If you wrote a song about self-love, list 4 titles that you would give it?

Date: ....

24. What is your funniest childhood memory?

25. What do you LOVE about your life right NOW?

....

....

....

....

....

....

....

....

Stay magical

Date: ....

26. How do you like spending time with your family?

1.
....
2.
....
3.
....
4.
....
5.
....
6.
....
7.
....

Date: ....

27. What are some fun things you like to do with your friends?

1.

2.

3.

4.

5.

6.

Date: ....

28. What are your favorite character traits and why?

I love to love

29. What is an instrument that you have always wanted to play that would bring you joy?

....

....

....

....

....

....

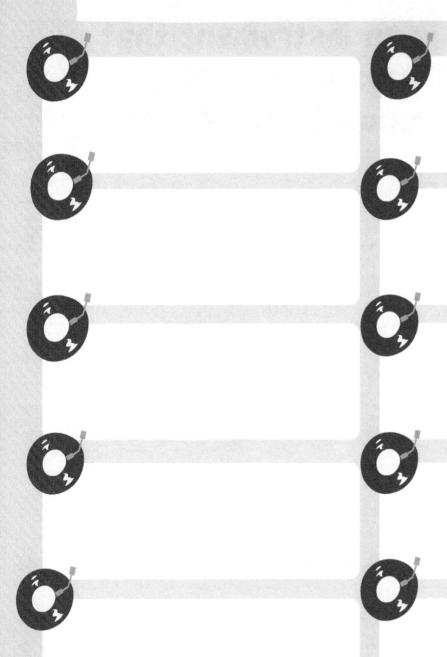

I
AM
······ Loving ······
AND
GENEROUS

31. What is your favorite music to listen to and why?

....

....

....

....

....

....

....

....

Date: ....

32. Three things that I am good at are...

1.

2.

I AM SO GRATEFUL

3.

I am ☆ That Girl

33. How does this music make you feel and what emotions move through your body?

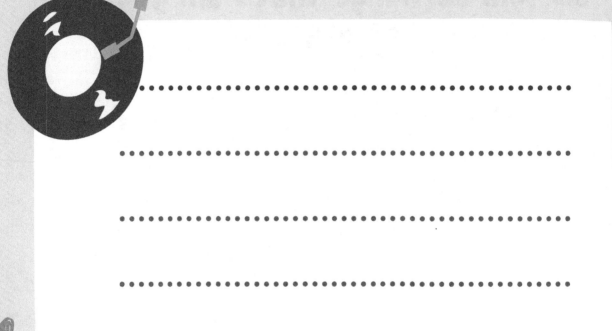

....

....

....

....

Here's how I feel after listening to music:

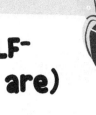

34. Create the lyrics to your SELF-LOVE song (no matter what they are) on the next 3 pages.

SONG TITLE

1

....

Add lyrics here

....

....

....

....

....

....

....

ADD MORE LYRICS

ADD MORE LYRICS

···

···

···

···

···

···

···

···

Date: ....

35. List 5 things you are grateful for today.

36. Create a bucket list of 5 things you want to do before the end of the year.

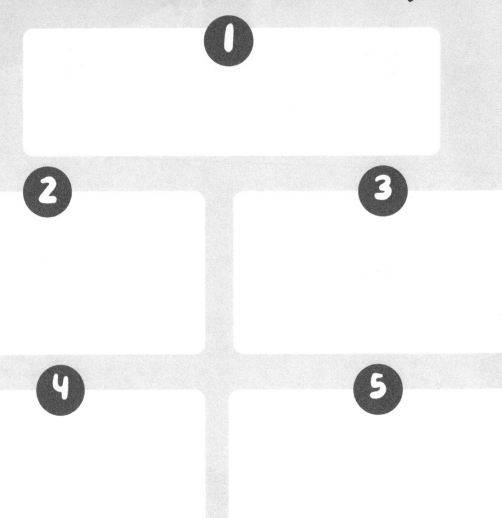

1

2

3

4

5

Date: ....

37. Write 7 kind words about the life you've had so far.

1.
....

2.
....

3.
....

4.
....

5.
....

6.
....

7.
....

38. What are some self-love quotes that inspire and motivate you?

1.

2.

3.

4.

5.

39. Make a list of people you look up to and why.

1

2

3

4

5

always
STAND UP
for your
BELIEFS

Date: ....

40. When I'm alone, I love to ...

_ _

_ _

_ _

_ _

_ _

_ _

_ _

_ _

_ _

MY FAV
BOOK IS

41. What is a recent book you read or are reading? What have you learned from this book?

....

....

....

....

....

....

....

....

42. What are your favorite SELF-LOVE affirmations?

#1

#2

#4

#5

Date: ....

43. What is the best compliment you have received? How did that make you feel?

....

....

....

....

....

....

....

44. The best thing about today is.........

Date: ....

45. What's one thing you have learned about life so far?

....

....

....

....

....

....

....

46. Is there a memory you wish you could re-live? What is it?

47. Name 3 things that make you UNIQUE.

1.

2.

3.

I bring peace

I am brave

48. If I had the power to change the world, I would ...

....

....

....

....

....

....

....

....

Date: ....

51. What are your favorite hobbies?

1.

2.

3.

4.

5.

6.

50. What is your idea of a perfect summer vacation?

Date: ....

51. If you could relive one school year, what year would that be and why?

_____

_____

_____

_____

_____

_____

_____

_____

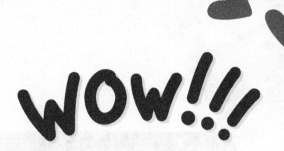

52. I was REALLY surprised when...

....

....

....

....

....

....

....

53. What are your top 5 goals for your school year?

1

2

3

4

5

Date: ....

54. Do you have any long-term goals? What are they?

1. ....

2. ....

3. ....

4. ....

5. ....

6. ....

55. Set a goal for yourself this month, no matter how small.

I WILL...

....

....

....

....

....

....

....

56. Write down a list of three things you will do to accomplish this goal.

1

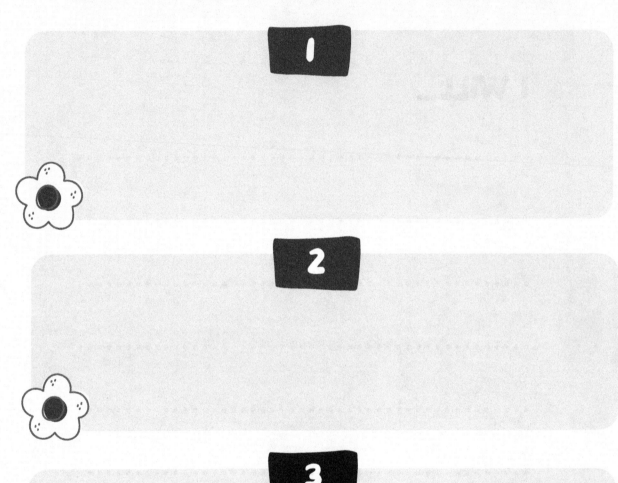

2

3

57. What music inspires you and why?

....

....

....

....

....

....

....

....

58. What are your TOP 3 favorite movies about self love?

1.

2.

3.

59. What are 5 things you are passionate about?

1

2

3

4

5

60. List 3 things that you do to show your family love.

1.

2.

3.

61. I make others feel loved by ...

_____

_____

_____

_____

_____

_____

_____

Date: ....

62. 7 Things that make me SMILE are:

1.
....

2.
....

3.
....

4.
....

5.
....

6.
....

7.
....

You're DOING great

Date: ....

63. Write about a special time when you helped someone.

----

64. List 5 things that you would say THANKS to yourself for...

1

2

3

4

5

BE YOUR
Best
SELF

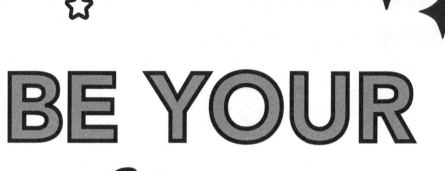

65. What are 3 things you've done to show yourself love?

1.

2.

3.

Date: ....

66. If you could take a trip to anywhere in the world, where would it be and why?

_____

_____

_____

_____

_____

_____

_____

_____

_____

67. I am worthy of happiness because...

....

....

....

....

....

....

....

....

....

....

68. I will tell myself these 5 affirmations everyday to show myself love:

1

2

3

4

5

Date: ....

69. Why do you think self love is important?

....

....

....

....

....

....

....

....

you're amazing

Date: ....

70. Why do you think self love is important?

_____

_____

_____

_____

_____

_____

_____

_____

71. I feel loved when I ...

....

....

....

....

....

....

....

....

72. Write down one self love goal for the year.

_____

_____

_____

_____

_____

_____

_____

73. What feature do you love MOST about your body?

Date: ....

74. What is your favorite animal and why?

....

....

....

....

....

....

Date: ....

75. What is your favorite thing about your personality?

....

....

....

....

....

....

....

....

76. Write a love letter to your future self on the next 2 pages!

_____

_____

_____

_____

_____

_____

_____

_____

_____

Date: ....

_____

_____

_____

_____

_____

_____

_____

_____

77. What is a hidden talent that you have?

....

....

....

....

....

....

....

....

Date: ....

78. What would you do if you were BRAVE?

Be
Brave

_____

_____

_____

_____

_____

_____

_____

_____

I am brave

79. What scary things would you like to do more of?

....

....

....

....

....

....

80. What new things have you learned this year that you want to do more of?

THE
END

Made in the USA
Las Vegas, NV
28 November 2023

81734640R00059